THE MENTAL CAPACITY OF UNSPOKEN THOUGHTS

THE MENTAL CAPACITY OF UNSPOKEN THOUGHTS

Lorraine Elise

THE PAPER HOUSE
PUBLISHING

Copyright © 2024 by Lorraine Ford

All rights reserved.

No part of this book may be reproduced in any form or by any electronic or mechanical means, including information storage and retrieval systems, without written permission from the author, except for the use of brief quotations in a book review.

Printed in the USA

Contents

   PROLOGUE   1
1. WRITE   3
2. MY OWN   5
3. MEMORY LANE   9
4. THE ROSE   11
5. STORM   13
6. LEFT BEHIND   15
7. WHAT IS DEPRESSION?   17
8. HAUNTED ATTRACTION   21
9. RESCUE STORY   23
10. FREEDOM   25
11. BUILT FROM FLAMES   27
12. FINALLY…   29
13. DARK WATERS   31
14. GRIEF   33
15. FICKLE   35
16. #1 FAN   37
17. LOVE ME TOO   39
18. NATURE   41
19. TEARS OF AN AUTHOR   43
20. CALL HER CRAZY   45
21. WILTED TIME   49
22. I UNDERSTAND   51
23. ARE YOU OKAY?   53
24. THANK YOU!   55
25. SO MANY STARS   57
26. NOT TODAY   59
27. JUST A DREAM   61
28. GRAY AREA   63
29. ALL THE THINGS I DIDN'T GET TO SAY   65

30. LAW OF THE TREES	67
31. I DRIFTED OUT TO SEA	69
32. MORE THAN A DOG	71
33. MUSICAL CHAIRS	73
34. THINGS I HATE ABOUT YOU	75
35. MY EULOGY	77
36. RIGHT PERSON, WRONG TIME	81
37. IN ANOTHER LIFE	83
38. CRY FOR HELP	85
39. INFIDELITY	87
40. YOU'RE STILL HERE, BUT I MISS YOU ALREADY	89
41. FEAR	91
42. HARLOW	93
43. REASONS	95
44. IDENTITY	97
45. BUTTERFLY EFFECT	99
46. PROMISES	101
47. CAROUSEL	103
48. ALL OF THEM - ALL OF YOU	105
49. SAVANNAH	107
50. WHY SO TIRED?	109
51. SO TINY	113
52. A WRINKLE IN TIME	115
53. IMPOSTER SYNDROME	117
54. NOT SO FRAGILE	119
55. MONSTER	121
56. BLENDED PAGES	123
57. SECRETS	125
58. DISTRACTION	127
59. MR. HAPPY	129
60. I BURY ALL MY CHILDREN	131
61. SILENT	133
62. DISASSOCIATE	135
63. OH HOW SHE LOVED HIM	137
64. CHOOSE	141

65.	HERE'S YOUR ANSWER	143
66.	TEASE	145
67.	MIRROR, MIRROR	147
68.	WHERE THERE'S SMOKE, THERE'S FIRE	149
69.	DON'T SAY	151
70.	WHERE DO WE GO?	153
71.	REMEMBER	157
72.	I'M SORRY	159
73.	ALL FOR NOTHING	161
74.	SELFISH DEMOLITION	163
75.	MY DAUGHTER	165
76.	ROAD TRIP	167
77.	A FAMILIAR PLACE	169
78.	CHECK MATE	173
79.	WE ALL BLEED	177
80.	I WONDER	181
81.	JAGGED MIND	183
82.	YOUR FINALE	185
83.	TRIALS OF A DOG	189
84.	HEAD IN THE CLOUDS	191
85.	WHERE DARKNESS LIES	193
86.	HABIT	197
87.	DREAM WORLD	199
88.	MY DESTINATION	201
89.	LOST AND FOUND	203
90.	FRENEMY	205
91.	THE WORST DAY OF MY LIFE	207
92.	I STUMBLE	209
93.	THE HUNT OF AN INNOCENT DEER	211
94.	SPIRITUAL WARFARE	213
95.	THE GIFT	215
96.	WALKING AMONG US	217
97.	DEATH IS NOT THE ANSWER	219
98.	THE PRINCESS AND THE WOLF	221

99. US AND THEM	223
100. ILLUSION	225

To My Mother:

You gave me the gift of strength, and because of that I was able to find the courage to tell my story. To never be ashamed of it. To thrive from it, shine a light on it, and to grow from it.

Thank you for being the foundation of my sanity and being a part of this journey with me.

To Agnes:

This book was created with the help of all your support. You pushed me every day to turn my words into a creation of something bigger. Thank you for always being my #1 fan.

PROLOGUE

Since I was a little girl, writing has always been an escape for me.

As the years passed on within time, it became one of my greatest passions.

When someone reads the words that come from my mind, then printed onto paper with the stroke of a pen, it became clear to me that some readers can relate.

Some people have so much on their mind, but can't find the words to put into existence. Having the opportunity to do that for them has always been a blessing.

Words mean everything.

They come from pain, come from truth, come from within.

Words have a way of impacting the brain either for the better or for the worse.

It's a release, a coping mechanism, an escape.

PROLOGUE

While reading these lines, please remember to also read in between them.

For they carry a message that once related to me, and hopefully some to you.

These words come from the heart, from pain, from trauma, from past, present and future thoughts.

You will read stories that are heartfelt, sensitive, cruel, scary, funny, and wise.

These words can be fun, delicate, rough, and even at times may seem raw.

I hope whoever picks up these pages gets to come on a journey with me.

Learn to laugh, learn to have an open mind, to cry, grow, heal, or to simply just listen.

So welcome everyone!

Welcome to my mind.

WRITE

You say you want to write, so write about your pain.

Write about your feelings.

Write about all the places your mind goes.

The places that are so deep most people are afraid to swim.

Write about the raw emotions that hide behind the eyes that show no transparency.

Write so deep that the reader gets cold ripples on their skin and a chill down their spine.

Write about your experiences, therefore some can relate.

For the reader to be so captivated they forget they are reading someone else's story and not their own.

And if you feel nothing, but numb, write about that.

Write about the deprived sensation.

Write about paralyzed emotion.

WRITE

Write about the silence.

Let the reader feel the same exact feeling you get when picking up the pen.

MY OWN

I was born into a world that intended to tear me apart.
To judge and use shame right from the start.

I didn't understand how easy it was to break a heart.
Then from the moment I did, life began to fall apart.

As a little girl I was hated for my skin.
They saw tan on the outside and then judged within.

With all the awful things said, my head would start to spin.
I grew up thinking being me was a sin.

People showed me a world that it can be a cruel place.

MY OWN

I had my own demons I started to face.

I hated my looks, my personality, my race.

Numbing myself was an option so I wanted a taste.

I was dishonest with myself because of the things I've allowed.

Did a lot of things for money, things I'm not proud.

Walked into a room to see all those men bow.

With all the drugs in my system, I was living on a cloud.

The things I saw, the things I did, I can list them in a book.

The ways I tried to hurt myself, cause I didn't like my looks.

Years of tears with drugs and beers.

Years of fear, but it all disappeared.

I got motivation, I found wisdom, and used that to thrive.

I got stronger and smarter. What a time to be alive.

I saw the shallow waters, but instead I just dived.

Everything I overcame, I did it and survived.

THE MENTAL CAPACITY OF UNSPOKEN THOUGHTS

When I was offered coke, yea I sniffed that.

I was handed a blunt, yea I hit that.

When I was hating myself, yea I got over that.

When I was sexually assaulted, yea I overcame that.

When I was verbally abused, shit I ate that.

Strong and my own hero, damn right I became that.

I had fire in my eyes, I started to feel strong.

For the first time in forever I felt like I belonged.

Everything I was told not to do, I turned around and did it.

Everything I was doubted from, I competed and I won it.

Because in life you can't just dream it.

If you feel it, and need it, then simply just do it.

It feels like forever, but a couple of years is what it took.

Now when I need to find a fighter, in the mirror I'll look.

Wait and be patient for what life brings.

Of course I fly, I grew my own wings.

Who became my vision and helped me see?

MY OWN

Who helped me grow and made it feel free?

There was never a "who" and never a "we".

The person who always helped that "who" was always me!

MEMORY LANE

Since you're not around anymore.

Very often awake or in bed.

I go to a place where I know you are,

It's a trip that I take in my head.

It's beautiful there and time don't exist,

Neither does sadness or pain.

Every time I go I always get to see you,

Because the place is called memory lane.

To hear the way you say my name,

Or how you sang to me.

The way you used to stroke my hair,

What I'd give to relive memories.

When I pass by your house,

I'd love to knock on your door.

MEMORY LANE

But, I know that you won't answer,

Cause you're not there anymore.

I hate the fact that you're not here.

After all these dreadful years.

Can you see me? Can you hear me?

Are you able to visit the moon?

All these questions that I have,

I guess I'll ask them soon.

It breaks my heart to ever think,

There's a chance I won't see you again.

To fully let go of your hands,

And say goodbye to my best friend.

I try as I walk, to hold my head high,

Life without you will never be the same.

So when I need to be with you,

I'll take a trip down memory lane.

THE ROSE

Have you ever smelt a rose,
Then fell in love with her bloom?

It was the way that she blossomed,
The smell of her perfume.

Soft as velvet,
When you brush against her pedals.

You watch her like the sun,
When she dances in the meadows.

You sat and gave her water.
Loved to watch her grow.

THE ROSE

To come back at midnight,
To watch the moonlight glow.

This rose you want for yourself,
So you decide to bend and pick her.

Went against its nature,
Her pollinate will die much quicker.

You disrupt her value of growth,
Mother Nature will start to mourn.

She cut you when you ripped her,
From the ground you forgot she's thorned.

STORM

Rolling rumbles of thunder.

Shrieking whistles from the wind.

Ombre darkness, arrival of clouds.

Excessive ripples pounding from the rain.

It's the storm I love to watch.

In the middle of the storm I want to be.

The lightning looks so beautiful.

Strobes of electricity in many forms.

I feel at peace from the sound of thunder.

I can feel the emotion of the storm.

Maybe it's the raindrops, or the whipping wind that I love.

It's the storm, who I understand.

The emotional breakdown from above.

STORM

I see the storm.

I hear the storm.

I feel the storm.

Maybe because I am the storm.

LEFT BEHIND

Broken, pain, death is what I feel.

Shattered, choking, I can never heal.

Vanished, alone, lost in mind.

Your memory is here, but I'd rather be blind.

You left and took all of what's yours and what's not.

But, there is something you left behind, something you forgot.

It's red, it's long, it's thick, it's perfect.

I'll wrap it around my neck, why not? I'm not worth it.

What's left is nothing, only me and how you felt.

What's left beside that, is your one and only belt.

Don't feel guilty, it's what you wanted all along.

An excuse to leave, an excuse to go home.

Clearly I'm not enough to fit where you belong.

LEFT BEHIND

So if you left then what's the difference if I'm dead, am I wrong?

The one thing you left behind helped me feel free.

Because now without you, there won't be me.

Blame yourself for leaving when you always knew the cost.

The love you left behind will now always be lost.

You left me alone in this house by myself.

You left me with nothing, nothing but your belt.

WHAT IS DEPRESSION?

Have you ever woke up grateful that you opened your eyes, but muddled that you're awake?

Have you ever walked into a room with a smile on your face, but know the smile's fake?

Have you ever felt the need to keep pushing just for survival sake?

Have you ever looked up to the sky and felt that you're not from this place?

Well same...

It's the feeling of contradiction with every thought that's made.

WHAT IS DEPRESSION?

It's the hope that holds on to memories, but the pain wants them to fade.

It's getting spurts of energy, yet fighting to stay awake.

It's being tired of constantly giving, yet never wanting to take.

To make plans with friends and family that you desperately want to keep.

But, as soon as the time comes around, all you want to do is sleep.

It's the feeling of being alone, but you know that's really not true.

It's the thought that everyone is happy, everyone of course except you.

The feeling of sanity, but then also feeling nuts.

The feeling of pain, but numb all at once.

It's the feeling of sadness with no explanation, where darkness goes to hide.

THE MENTAL CAPACITY OF UNSPOKEN THOUGHTS

It's the feeling of trying to constantly catch up, yet somehow you always fall behind.

It's the feeling of worry about past, present, and future, the nagging questions of why.

It's the feeling of wanting to live, but in the same breath also wanting to die.

HAUNTED ATTRACTION

Halloween is the time to get spooked and scared.

A haunted house to enter, It's a horror state fair.

Enter the Haunted house, but it's best to go at night.

Inside there's no mercy, no light and no sight.

Your heart beats rapidly, sweat starts to fall.

Hear nothing, but your footsteps walking through the hall.

With every step you take you'll often hear a creek.

But, the sound is from poltergeist not from your feet.

You go deeper as you walk and end in a cave.

You see a dark hole with dirt and your name on a grave.

HAUNTED ATTRACTION

There's nowhere to run, you're already in a box.
There's a soft pad under you, but the box is fully locked.

Panic sets in and you start to lose your breath.
It's coming for you and it sounds like death.

Your eyes are taped closed and your heart loses its beat.
You can't move anymore, not your hands nor your feet.

It's tragic when you become a victim, but it happens very often.
We need the bodies for display to put in our coffins!

RESCUE STORY

To you she's just a body, just a dog on the floor.

To me she's filled with love and worth so much more.

She gave you all her love, all her attention and respect.

All you gave her was a treat, and nothing, but neglect.

She wagged her puppy tail, and came to you for fetch.

All you had to offer was a life that she'll forget.

You wasted all her years, you should be so lucky.

You got the time to spend with her, since she was a puppy.

But, luck was not her favor, luck was never handed.

You took the love she gave you and you took it all for granted.

You said that it got rough, and I said that it's okay.

But, we had to come and take her so she could live another day.

RESCUE STORY

You said that it was challenging, but you still couldn't see.

All the wrong you know you did, and why you gave her up to me.

I had to set her free, I know you really tried.

But, trying wasn't enough anymore, I cried and cried and cried.

Her tail is finally wagging. Again she can be,

Happy with a family, who makes her a priority.

All the things you did to her, you won't face it, nor want to hear it.

You may have broken her home, but you will never break her spirit.

She can bark with all the joy, play with toys, and get to dance.

We rescued her from hell, so she can have another chance.

FREEDOM

Do as we suppose, work until we die.

Follow the rules blindly, until all of us will rise.

Born on a floating rock, but to survive we must work.

It doesn't matter where you're from, if you're smart, woke, or hurt.

Where expected to make money, not for the poor, but for the rich.

So they can throw you a stick that can barely scratch your itch.

Till one of us woke up, then started waking others.

Women are expected to provide, become wives, and also mothers.

FREEDOM

When a man can't work two jobs to make enough to provide his family.

Prices going up, but not our pay, only your insanity.

Then they wonder why we rebel against the country financially.

They want to take as much as possible and show us no humanity.

Using our tax dollars, to fund NASA in building rockets.

So they can escape the planet they're killing, while digging in our pockets.

Civilians were uniting, you won't take from us no more.

When it comes to our freedom, we prepare for war.

We were taught that we are free, on our own and independent.

Our leaders became our enemy, which is why we practice our second amendment.

We'll come together, but we'll fight for what's right and wrong for all.

We will fight for all our freedom, even if together we all fall.

BUILT FROM FLAMES

If you knew how tough I was,

You would be shocked by how I recovered.

With all the ups and downs,

And the healing I found, it was bravery I had to discover.

I crawled through the flames,

I'm no stranger to hell.

But, I handled what life threw at me,

And I handled it so well.

I don't fear walking in the dark.

That's how I'm mechanically wired.

I was tossed to the sparks.

But, came out wearing the fire.

Struggle was just my enemy,

BUILT FROM FLAMES

Not where I belonged.

I came out on top,

Because my middle name is strong.

FINALLY...

You don't even know,
What I'm about to do.

Remember that medicine you fed me?
Now I'm feeding you!

Can't wait to see your expression.
I hope you're really shook.

I can't wait for your lesson.
I took a page from your book.

I will move in silence,
Like you've never seen before.

FINALLY...

You won't see it coming,
When I walk out that door.

I gave so many chances.
Had so many hopes.

I held on so ever tightly,
To those fraying ropes.

I wanted you to care.
But, care you really don't.

So I hope I break your heart.
And I hope that you won't cope.

You dragged me through the mud.
Wasted year after year.

I can't wait for you to hurt.
When I finally disappear.

DARK WATERS

Her mind was deep like water.
But too deep for people to swim.
The deeper you got, the closer you came,
To the secrets she's kept within.
At times the water seemed different.
Not too deep, but rather shallow.
Those times her heart would sing a song.
So high they called it soprano.
But, not many wanted that tune.
It was only meant for the brave.
To dare to care, or dare to swim,
Against her rapid waves.
Her mind stood deep waiting for the one,
That was ready to hop on boat.

DARK WATERS

To find her depth so beautiful,

They didn't mind to sink, and not float.

GRIEF

Losing a loved one is never easy.

We often associate our grief with never seeing that loved one again.

But, that is simply not true.

Death is both a blessing and a curse.

A curse to the ones who are left behind to mourn with sadness.

To leave us behind with questions like why? Or what ifs.

But, death is also a blessing to the ones who are passing on.

Though they are not leaving us forever, but only moving on to a higher realm.

Better than here, better than what we call home.

Death comes to take us home to where we truly belong.

They are not physically here, but spiritually here.

Parallel to our existence, just on another plane.

So if you ever think you won't get the chance to see them again, please have second thoughts.

As they have the blessing to be here, there, and everywhere,

All at once.

And just like them, one day….

So will we.

FICKLE

Your love is never consistent, and because of that, neither is my mood.

You love me one day, and the next day I'm lucky if I even exist.

The days that you love me are the days you're on my team.

Those are the days where I come first.

Those are the days I matter to you most, when it's just me and you against the world.

Those days you make me feel unstoppable, make me feel safe, make me feel secure, make me feel loved.

But, on the days I barely exist, you don't speak to me, and if you do it's always monotone.

Those days you stare at me with empty eyes and an empty heart.

Those are the days you can care less if you ever knew me at all.

FICKLE

Those days you make me feel worthless, unimportant, and unloving.

Those days you make me feel invisible for how you look right through me.

So now I'm worried.

I'm worried about what kind of day I'm going to wake up to tomorrow.

Will you love me?

Or will you just tolerate me?

I hope to wake up one day and realize I can't do this anymore.

But, I'm worried that day will never come.

It will be your unstable emotions that will eventually break me.

#1 FAN

Born with a brain that has the capacity to receive and understand endless knowledge.

The ability to create, the ability to rebuild, the ability to destroy.

Have the understanding that we instinctively do what we need to do to survive.

While simultaneously also having the potential to destroy our very own selves.

The heart and brain are meant to work together, but often turn feelings into a challenge.

Our emotions take residence in our hearts, but our intelligence lives in the brain.

Emotions are powerful and can come off strong, but don't let it conquer your intelligence.

Emotions get you hurt.

Intelligence helps you heal.

We forget we need to take care of ourselves, not just physically but mentally as well.

While we repeatedly search for acceptance in others, we forget to accept ourselves.

We push ourselves aside, forgetting it's important to be your personal number one fan.

We take life's important lessons then beat ourselves up when we make common, reasonable mistakes.

Water ourselves down till our mental stability overflows.

Then get upset when we emotionally drown.

We control our own reality, we are the creators to our life's game.

We become our own enemy, but learn to defeat it so we can receive the prize of peace.

Peace is unreachable until you accept the lessons you have to experience and face.

Lessons can be cruel, but they are necessary.

We're meant to be open, learn, grow, and evolve, in order for us to ascend.

Take care of yourself. Nurture your needs so in your next destination you can advance.

Every day you wake up and open your eyes, you're given another chance.

LOVE ME TOO

I love you, but I have to love me too.

I had to learn to love myself, this way I can properly love.

It all went wrong because you didn't know how to love yourself when you needed to most.

Everything you hated about yourself you took it out on me.

You reflected your pain and made me feel the same.

I was willing to share that pain to help ease your burden, and you destroyed me in the process.

But, I couldn't blame you.

How could you properly love me, when you didn't know how to love yourself?

LOVE ME TOO

The more that time passed, the more I couldn't recognize myself when I looked into the mirror.

You were taking away my happiness, you were taking away my spirit.

You took it all away when I was trying to help you find yours.

I didn't want to let you go, but I had to let you go, for the sake of all you put me through.

I love you, but I have to love me too.

NATURE

I'm happiest most,

When I'm centered in the trees.

When my feet are crunching,

Against fallen leaves.

I feel most at peace,

When I'm one with the sky.

Watching the birds,

Stretch their wings set to fly.

The animals are my friends,

And the moon is my light.

It hides during the day,

But, it protects me most at night.

The sun keeps me warm,

When I'm quick to shiver.

NATURE

I replenish my thirst,

By drinking the river.

When I need cleansing,

I take a dip in the pond.

We share a relation,

A very special bond.

I'm the closest to the stars,

When they shine in the water.

Mother Nature has much to offer,

I feel like her daughter.

She kisses me with raindrops,

And hugs me with the wind.

I hear her voice in my ear,

And her touch on my skin.

I jump from rocks to mountains,

Feet touching granite.

I think I'm made of stardust,

A part of the planet.

I wondered about my purpose.

What am I worth?

I have a connection,

But, only one with the earth.

TEARS OF AN AUTHOR

Do you know their story?

Or why they wrote their book?

You judged them by the cover,

By only viewing looks.

Did you get to read the back?

To overview and learn the summary?

Do you know how they were saved?

Did they make it through recovery?

Was their story written in pencil?

Or did they write in pen?

Is there room to erase mistakes?

Did you make it to the end?

Did you read the details?

Or just flip through the chapters?

TEARS OF AN AUTHOR

You judged by reading briefly,

Ignoring all the factors.

Did you skim through the pages?

Or read between the lines?

Did you feel each word embroidered,

Or brush your finger down the book's spine?

Just like every book, it will fade when it's in water.

It faded because of tears that poured out from the author.

As readers often do, grab it off the shelf and barely look.

Before fully reading the important plot that makes the author's book.

CALL HER CRAZY

When we first met,

I spoke about how fragile my heart was.

I shared my hesitation on letting you in.

You begged for vulnerability,

Even when I told you I wasn't ready.

I was not ready to give you the opportunity to break me.

But, in time you showed me I can trust you.

That I could leap into your arms knowing they were open to catch me.

We sat for hours and I spoke my truth.

Only for you to gather that information to one day use against me.

When I least expected it, you had the barrel of my gun pointing at my back, never my face.

It was easier for you that way.

CALL HER CRAZY

Easier for you to feed me your poison slowly.

Slowly enough for me to not realize you have been killing me all along.

When the gun is pressed on my back,

I turn to you to scream.

But, you call me crazy.

I come to you with solutions to fix our problems.

But, I'm too emotional, too loud,

And you call me crazy.

I hold in my tears until they become outburst.

And when I burst you call me crazy.

I'm crazy for being upset.

Upset that I gave you the instructions on how to break my heart.

But, I don't think you know what crazy really is.

Crazy is not defending my sanity.

Crazy is not addressing your wrongs.

Crazy is not fighting for my happiness.

Crazy is not setting boundaries.

I guess if I'm crazy then crazy can be justified.

I saw you play your game and used your pieces against you.

Stole the poison you fed me to start feeding you.

Planted a chip in your head to let you think you own me.

THE MENTAL CAPACITY OF UNSPOKEN THOUGHTS

And when you least expect it, flip the script the one you showed me.

This crazy girl played you, left you astonished and stumped.

My words became the noose around your neck that made you jump.

You picked me as a flower thinking you were getting a daisy.

But, this daisy had teeth and now you call her crazy.

WILTED TIME

Holding on to someone who you have hope for, can be more damaging then letting them go.

You hold on to them for so long with the anticipation that maybe one day, some day, they will finally love you for how you're supposed to be loved.

Maybe they will, but most of the time they won't.

Taking a gamble on your own happiness for someone else's realization, will only make you realize one day that you did nothing, but waste your time.

By the time that day comes you would have missed dozens of opportunities to possibly meet someone who would love you for how you always wanted to be loved.

One day when that person you have been holding on to finally comes to terms on how they feel, it will be then when they themselves realize you were never the one they wanted to love all along.

So, let them go.

WILTED TIME

Go find your happiness while they find whatever they are searching for.

Before it becomes nothing, but wasted years.

I UNDERSTAND

They see you as a monster, someone who is scary.

But, I see that's how you were molded, so I don't think you're so scary at all.

They hear you yell and fear your roar.

But, I hear your bellow and feel your fear.

They don't understand you, and if they can, they won't.

But, I understand you, cause I witnessed your creation.

I understand that children who experience trauma can grow up complicated from how they were wired.

I understand the difficult trials you had to experience, and your data was programmed so poorly.

They don't understand and won't understand that your creation was created by a dark entity.

I understand your creation and all the complications that created this so-called monster.

I UNDERSTAND

They may see darkness, but I see your light, trust me, I wish they also could.

I see a little boy hiding from his monster, who wishes the others understood.

ARE YOU OKAY?

I'm not okay.

How could I be okay when the world around me is falling apart?

I see everyone walking around with smiles on their faces, with not a care in the world.

Yet, when I turn on social media all I see is destruction.

When I was a little girl, I couldn't wait to grow up.

Now that I'm grown I wish I can go back to being a child.

Pain, there is so much pain.

Around me, in me.

I cannot turn this pain off.

Even if it is not mine.

I see too much, hear too much, feel too much, fear too much.

All of this because the world became too much…

THANK YOU!

I want to please and thank you,
For all the things you didn't.

I want to thank you for your love,
Even though you only hid it.

Thank you for all the lies,
And for the ones that I saw coming.

Thank you for asking me to stay,
When I really should be running.

Thank you for standing next to me,
When you were never on my side.

THANK YOU!

Thank you for all the headaches,
With heartbreaks that waste my time.

Thank you for opening up your prison,
When you were supposed to be my home.

But, thank god I'm only thirty,
And you'll be my stepping stone.

Thank you for all the drama,
For every tear, and every fight.

Thank you so much for becoming a topic,
That helps my fame to get to write.

SO MANY STARS

She walked around with mystery,

And he would often wonder.

What caused her rain, and her pain,

Her lightning, and her thunder.

He wanted to know her story,

To read the chapters in her book.

His desperation to get to know her,

With every chance it took.

As seasons began to pass,

Their relationship would grow.

As he read her pages,

The more he got to know.

He got to read her story,

But sure she hid the damage.

SO MANY STARS

With long sleeves set to cover,

The band aids and the bandage.

They laid arm in arm,

Looking up at the stars.

He thought there were so many,

Until he saw her arms.

NOT TODAY

I got on the scale today.

But, before I did I made sure to take off every layer.

And if I did good, but only to my liking,

I can eat and treat myself later.

Socks come off too.

It's a standard routine, Important for every appointment.

Can't have anything contribute or add onto

My next upcoming disappointment.

If I gained an extra pound,

Was it because I over ate?

NOT TODAY

Maybe the portions were too heavy.
Next time I'll use a smaller plate.

The scale shows a lower number,
I close my eyes and huff.

But not a release, more like a pout.
The number I see is not enough.

I will just settle for water this week.
It's the price I have to pay.

Even if it kills me.
I don't deserve to eat today.

Not today
Not today
Not today
Until I shrivel away.

JUST A DREAM

I had a dream last night. It felt so real.

I wish it was.

I got to hold you in my arms, which I never thought would happen.

As short of a time as I've known you, I seem to love you forever.

I can still smell the soft baby scent that whiffs off your head when I reach down to kiss it.

I have been trying for years to have this experience.

But, experiencing you was never in my deck of cards.

Though I only held you for a short while, my arms still aspire to hold your little body.

To hear your little laugh, to look down with watered eyes, to see your beautiful baby smile.

Thank you my little girl.

JUST A DREAM

Thank you for letting me be your mother, even if it was only for a short while.

Even if it was only just a dream.

Just a dream, I wish I didn't have to wake up from.

GRAY AREA

If you ask me a question, I guarantee you won't receive a simple answer.

Ask me my favorite color, my answer won't be simple.

Depending on the texture, or the item the color is on. I like many different colors, for many different things.

Ask me who I like better, cats or dogs? My answer won't be simple.

I will give you pros and cons of each, but I'll say I love them both.

Ask what's my favorite food? My answer won't be simple.

I will ask which type of meal you are referring to, since I love so many dishes.

GRAY AREA

Ask me what's my favorite candy? My answer won't be simple.

I will ask which kind of candy? Sweet? Gummy? Chocolate? Or sour?

Ask me my opinion on a situation involving different people. My answer won't be simple.

I will agree with one person, but also understand the other.

I don't see everything as simple as black and white.

I see reasons, I understand the variety of different sides.

I can see and understand the different points of views.

I believe in context.

I believe in diving deep.

I believe in tone.

I believe in roots and deeper meanings.

So, no, I'm not simple.

The questions you ask will be followed up with more questions than answers.

I don't believe everything can be black and white.

I live for the gray areas.

ALL THE THINGS I DIDN'T GET TO SAY

If I had a list of all the things I didn't get to say, the list would be pretty long.

That might come as a shock to others, knowing how outspoken I am.

Though that might be very true, there is plenty I hold back, plenty I don't say.

There have been people in my life where I felt I didn't get the opportunity to share the things I wanted to say to them.

But, the truth is, opportunity always existed.

It was the bravery for not caring of being judged for what I needed to speak into existence is what I was lacking.

Or all those times I wanted to put myself out there and say what I felt in my heart, but it was the fear of rejection that was preventing me from doing so.

ALL THE THINGS I DIDN'T GET TO SAY

There were times I wanted to stand up for myself when others have put me down and made me feel small. But, the anxiety from confrontation would shove my words down far enough to swallow.

So, yea, I'm outspoken. But, it wasn't always like that.

It took years to build myself up to say what I feel.

Even though I do, I still have limitations.

What felt like was only a short while ago, it was only till then when I found my voice.

LAW OF THE TREES

When you go for a hike, you think it's the animals that might find you and attack.

But, haven't you heard of people going missing, they enter, but never come back.

Does it have to do with creatures of the wild, or the secrets that lie in dirt?

But, you would never guess that the threat is in the trees, where the darkness lurks.

When the leaves blow from the wind, it's their mechanism for hissing.

No one ever questions the trees, when it's the people that go missing.

They blame the wild animals for bodies filling graves.

LAW OF THE TREES

They search the waters, search the grounds, search the trails and search the caves.

But, what do you get when you search and find nothing, no teeth, not even bone?

The disappearance of many in the Smoky Mountains, the Grand, and Yellowstone.

So you don't lose your way, you keep tracks on the trees, by making colorful marks.

But, you're marking up the culprit that is the real reason, people go missing in national parks.

We all have laws, when we take we must give, even from the grounds underneath.

I bet you didn't know that branches felt hunger, and the leaves that grow have teeth.

They crave what we owe them, their mouth is watering, the sap is their way to drool.

So we give them what they want, as nature we owe it, there has always been the unspoken rule.

We take from it, but give back to them, as nature needs to feed.

The balance of earth, we all must follow.

It's called the law of the trees.

I DRIFTED OUT TO SEA

I got tired of the familiar roads.

I grew bored with the same routine.

I yearned for the mysteries of adventure.

So, I decided to drift out to sea.

I jumped in my boat with no paddles.

Let the water take me adrift.

Escape the obedience of life.

I wonder what I'll miss.

I float in open water, as deep as the wonders of what the ocean contains.

I became so used to the sea, now it's the place that bores me.

My stability is crashing like waves.

I thought I needed change, but I'm not feeling so well.

I DRIFTED OUT TO SEA

Can't call for help to rescue, there's no service from a shell.

Found the grass is much greener, when your feet can touch the floor.

But, I wandered way too far, now I'm too far from the shore.

I drifted to feel bigger, but I never felt much smaller.

My face became so salty from my tears and all the water.

Took my everyday life for granted, now I'm stranded counting stars.

I drifted out to sea, but I drifted way too far....

MORE THAN A DOG

They give us love unconditionally.

They protect us.

Accept us.

Always are there for us.

Make us smile, make us laugh, for all the times we are upset.

They provide us companionship in this world, whether we are alone or not.

They never ask for much, only to love them back.

Whenever we need a hand, they give us a paw.

Whenever we need a kiss, they give us a lick.

Whenever we need to talk, they tilt their head to listen.

They give us all they have, so why not give them all we can offer?

We depend on them as much as they depend on us.

MORE THAN A DOG

Though they are only here for a short while.

They stay in our hearts forever.

They make us feel whole, when our reflection is broken.

This is why they deserve to share our voice, to speak for the unspoken.

MUSICAL CHAIRS

Be Careful with people who are desperate for attention and repel loneliness.

Those are the same type of people who will bash you for the relationship you have with others, then play the perfect game of musical chairs.

They can't wait for you to get up, just so they can take your seat.

THINGS I HATE ABOUT YOU

I hate how you put everyone's needs first and put mine last.

I hate how often you are willing to spend your last dollar to help everyone around you, but when the time comes that I need it, you don't have it.

I hate the way you forgive others so easily, but can't forgive me for reasonable mistakes.

I hate how much you can see everyone's worth besides mine.

I hate the way you build them up, but I can crumble and you wouldn't bat an eye.

THINGS I HATE ABOUT YOU

I hate how you keep yourself awake trying to help others put their puzzle pieces together, while mine have been missing and never found.

I hate the way you look into the mirror directly into our eyes knowing you put everyone else first before the one who's looking back at you.

MY EULOGY

We're all gathered here today not because of death, but because of life. What life had to offer was nothing, but the gift of death. I was young, full of impossible hope, filled with love, but also anger. And with that anger grew confusion. But, love, anger, and confusion is not what broke me. Not a man, not my family, not my past. Oh no, nothing like that at all. But, what had broken me was just life. I say the gift of death because I never believed death was the end. To me death was just a way to explain to someone that their time on earth [this planet, floating in the galaxy] has come to an end, and your soul is needed elsewhere. You leave your human shell here on earth and your energy, your spirit, your shadow, your real self will move on to a higher plane. A higher place where it will all finally start making sense.

Death is not the end. There is after life, there are theories of realms, and other endless possibilities to what only our small minds can't comprehend. But we will eventually. You hold on to your beliefs as a way of healing, as a way to cope with the fear of the unknown.

MY EULOGY

And you will have people scream science in your face over and over again. But, those people are here to make your faith stronger, to make you believe harder. The feeling of excitement that once this is all over, they will finally understand. We have experienced mediums, spirits coming through with messages, paranormal, and extraterrestrial existence. We have seen things we can't explain, heard things we can't explain, feel things we can't explain. And science will scratch their heads and go to eternity trying to find the scientific explanation as to why these things happen. But, guess what? The reason why science can't figure it out, is because science was created by humanity and we are so much more than that.

People tend to say the gift of life, but to me life was no gift. Life was a realm I couldn't understand. A planet that was so beautiful, so scary, so breathtaking. I couldn't understand how it could be so wrong. And it took me a while to realize that it's not the planet's fault. It's no one's fault but ourselves... humans. Humans destroy everything they touch and have the audacity to blame God, question God. Well if God is real why would they let this happen? Look around. All I see is crying humans wanting change, but they wipe their tears with their dirty hands, as if they didn't have a part in it. Some of us, a lot of us, most of us, like me, are dying to see change because we had so little to offer, but tried to offer all we had. Just to see people who can offer so much more, give so little, or hardly anything at all. I spent years walking around this existence holding back tears of pain. For someone so caring, so empathetic, had to experience such a cold fucked up world. That's why I left, that's why I had to say goodbye. To move on to a better realm. One that is meant for me. I get to finally get the gift I've always dreamt of, one that will lead me to endless possibilities. One that will allow me to see my loved ones again. One that I will finally have a purpose for. I'm ready to experience so much more now. I'm ready for the unknown.

RIGHT PERSON, WRONG TIME

Timing is everything, but when it comes to time, it's something we couldn't have.

Both are entwined in situations at the wrong time, with other halves.

At night we have our own worlds, which are separate until the day.

The sun comes up and from 9-5 you are mine till we part ways.

I want you to be happy, but who the hell am I kidding?

That's a lie I tell myself, maybe you'll get the joke I'm telling.

I was happy this whole time, well so I thought till I met you.

But, I'm already taken and in love, didn't know it was possible to now love two.

As much as I want to bid on the fruit that is very much forbidden.

RIGHT PERSON, WRONG TIME

We can't go on, as both of us have a story that has already been written.

A dream that stays a dream, only real till I awake.

If I had to count on it, you were my best one undone mistake.

We both got off the ride.

Because our worlds can never collide.

It hurts to say goodbye.

To a guy who was never mine.

IN ANOTHER LIFE

This life is filled with chaos,
Sadness, death and loss.
We suffer so much emptiness.
We kneel to pray to the cross.
If I could create another life,
There's so many things I'd do.
We wouldn't deal with loss,
So I won't be losing you.
There wouldn't be no questions,
This life would have the answer.
Medicine would not be needed
And this world would have no cancer.
Sickness won't become your enemy.
You wouldn't have to leave.

IN ANOTHER LIFE

The air would feel so heavenly,

You'll be as free to breathe.

You would watch me grow,

And help me raise my kids.

All the things you could have done,

If you only lived.

We would not have to stress a death,

You and I would be together.

Cause in this other life,

You would live forever.

CRY FOR HELP

When we often seek help, we seek in subtle ways.

I tried to be discreet without using the reluctant phrase.

The word help seems difficult, very close to needy.

I tried to ask the question without sounding greedy.

I dropped hint after hint, but you stood so silent.

You ignored my needs and made me feel reliant.

I asked for solutions to my problems, I wanted a fix.

I came for advice, but your withdrawal was a hint.

My problems were too much, I needed help to cope.

I was hanging on for life, but you seemed to drop the rope.

You left me alone, wondered astray.

I asked you to stay, but you turned and walked away.

I tried to ask for help, you wanted no part of my troubles.

CRY FOR HELP

So I sat alone with no worth, while drowning in my struggles.

No one in sight, not one single person.

I was left to feel like I was a burden.

So I decided to leave, to end my struggles for certain.

My show came to an end, the finale, closing the curtain.

It's real, I'm gone, it's too late now.

You ignored my signs, you ignored my sound.

When I was looking for you, you were nowhere to be found.

When I said I was falling, I already hit the ground.

INFIDELITY

I know it's me that you want, I can see it in your lies.

I put my hand on your arm, and your pulse begins to rise.

I know what you want, to take me for a test ride.

To boost your own ego, to fu-fill your own sex drive.

I know how to fill your needs, so I bat my big doe eyes.

Wear my hair slicked back, with tights that grip my thighs.

You whisper sweet sexy nothings, down into my ear.

I hand you the wheel, but I'm in charge of the gear.

I use my tease as keys, to lower your walls.

Then down on your knees, you come when I call.

Can't wait to have your way with me, watching the clock by the hour.

But, I let the time pass by because I hold that power.

INFIDELITY

The power of you, the power of my body.

A price you get to pay, for coming off so cocky.

Did you really think I'd let you treat me like a hobby?

To hop in my lap, rev me up like a Ferrari.

You're counting all your steps, when I'm already far ahead.

You thought my legs would spread, and you would end up in my bed.

You see me as a treat, but I played you like a trick.

The justice on my tongue, I bet you want a lick.

Life's famous quote "All good things come to an end".

I guess you didn't realize, I made your wife my friend.

YOU'RE STILL HERE, BUT I MISS YOU ALREADY

The circle of life.

A gift we are given that could make us feel so much sadness.

We are taught that with life, there is always death.

I understood since I was a child that dogs unfortunately don't live as long as humans do.

Being an animal lover I knew pain would be a price I would have to pay.

But, losing my dog is something I will never be ready for.

I wake up with you next to me every single day.

But, I already miss you even though you're still here.

I stare at you now, but I already can't wait to see you again.

YOU'RE STILL HERE, BUT I MISS YOU ALREADY

I look down at your bowls and cry knowing one day I will have to pick them up and put them away.

I see you laying in your favorite spot on my bed and sob for when the day comes when your spot will be empty.

I drive with you on my lap and see you squint as the wind hits your face.

And I already miss seeing you so happy.

You keep me company and are by my side every single day.

But, I miss your absence that will take place one day in the dreaded future.

I come home and open the door to see you happily greet me.

But, when I open the door, I know one day I'm going to walk into an empty home without you in it.

I try my best to not think about the day where you leave my world.

I guess it's in hopes to prepare myself for the worst thing that could ever happen to me.

But, nothing will ever prepare me.

No matter how much I grieve your existence, for when you no longer exist in this world.

Even though you are still here, I miss you already.

FEAR

I'm scared of death, but I'm not afraid to die.

I'm scared of who it will take away from me.

At any moment, in any time.

I'm worried about the heartache I will constantly have to carry for the remainder of time I exist.

Knowing the rest of my existence will now be in a world without them.

Knowing that I'm going to witness my loved ones leave this earth one by one and there is nothing I can do to prevent it.

Knowing I'm going to have to relive that pain over and over again.

Until my existence no longer exists in this memorable world forever.

HARLOW

Living without you is tough, I didn't want to try it.

I'm used to hearing your sounds, but now it's so quiet.

This house feels empty, it doesn't seem right.

You used to feel heavier, now you feel so light.

Sometimes I hear you purr, but I know it's the grief that mocks.

You used to sit in my lap, now you sit here in this box.

I can no longer see you, and though you're far away.

I carry you with me, I have you every day.

I stand in the kitchen, and feel you brush against my leg.

I asked God not to take you, trust me…I begged.

You were taken from me early, sooner than ever expected.

I memorialized your ashes, in a box with your toys collected.

HARLOW

You filled my life with love, gave me something I never thought I'd need.

But, now you're gone, as my heart sinks, I pray you come back to me.

In the meantime I'll still talk to you, as I look up at the stars.

Until the day I cross the same bridge, and you jump into my arms.

REASONS

You may not understand,

Why I became a writer.

The chance to express all the feels,

And to view perspectives wider.

The courage to speak out,

On all that occurred.

To glide my pen in style,

To finish all my words.

When writing became blocked,

It's my mind that I fought.

The struggle to get out,

A trapped frenzied thought.

To read all the readers,

Who can't sleep at night.

REASONS

It's then when it matters,

The reasons why I write.

IDENTITY

Who are you?

Don't tell me your name, or your age, or your height.

I don't want to hear about your positive traits or your humble characteristics.

Don't list all your favorite movies and books, nor explain what hobbies make you look interesting.

I don't want to know the basic borderline options your taste buds like to eat or drink.

I want to know who you are.

I want to know the thoughts that whirlpool in your mind when the rest of the world is asleep.

I want to know your day dreams when you gaze off into the distance looking through everyone and no one.

I want to know the nightmares that wake you up in a sweat that your fear doesn't want to remember.

I want to hear about your pain.

IDENTITY

I want to hear the trauma that made you who you are today.

I want to listen to the stories of how you overcame the obstacles that were challenging, yet you still survived.

I want to know the secrets you keep, even the darkest ones, so I can show you you're not alone.

I want to know how you feel about yourself when you look into the mirror when no one is around.

I want to know your shadow, more than I do your light.

I want to know your energy, the person who you are without skin, without a heart, without a vessel.

I want to know your soul.

I want to know the hidden parts of you that make you who you really are.

So tell me...

Who are you?

BUTTERFLY EFFECT

Of course I drowned in my struggles, but I coughed up the water and survived.

There have been times I choked, got burned, have fallen, and collapsed.

There were times I just laid there waiting to perish, but every single time, I got back up.

How could we appreciate happiness without experiencing sadness?

How could we know what love is without experiencing heartbreak?

How could we enjoy the sun without undergoing the rain?

How could we love the light without ever knowing the dark?

BUTTERFLY EFFECT

If I were to go back in time and change even the smallest thing to not face a struggle, I would not be where I am today.

I would not have what I have today.

I would not love who I love today.

I would not be who I am today.

If I was able to change it, who knows, maybe I would have a different outcome in my life.

But, it is not guaranteed.

That is something I would not be willing to gamble with.

So, I look around at my life with all its ups and downs, but there is a smile on my face.

I am grateful for it all!

Only until we experience the worst, is then when we can fully appreciate the best.

PROMISES

When promises break, it's the betrayal that hurts the most.

It's like trusting the medicine will work, without reading the deadly dose.

You put your faith into others, close your eyes and hope the best.

But, in reality your heart's the game, and the opponent is playing chess.

They say I'm the one that got away, but if they only knew that I escaped.

I had to jump to get away, to save my heart from endless scrapes.

I thought I was fighting for love, but I was fighting the wrong things.

I was holding onto you, and one by one you cut the strings.

PROMISES

When I asked for reassurance you said you gave so many.

When I asked you not to break me, you claimed to put me down gently.

When I asked for the bare minimum, you said you gave me plenty.

Then how come this pain I feel so densely?

Then how come when I look down, my hands are empty?

You sold me all those lies, till my heart was eventually ready.

Never realizing what I bought that night would be so fucking deadly.

We were on different pages, when we made promises that day.

I promised you my loyalty, and you promised me betray.

CAROUSEL

I'm tired.

I'm tired of the carousel heartache.

Up and down.

Repeat spin after spin.

I'm not the child sitting upon the ponies back,

Riding, having fun, and smiling.

I do not have the option to get off whenever I want to.

No!

I am the horse itself.

A pipe through my back holding me in place.

Forced to spin round and round.

This horse is tired.

I want to roam and flee.

Graze in the field.

CAROUSEL

And be what a horse is meant to be.

Free...

ALL OF THEM - ALL OF YOU

They all want me.

They tell me how beautiful I am.

Gush over me.

Tell me all the things I wish to hear from you.

They appreciate me.

They value me.

They lift me up when you put me down.

They make me laugh.

They make me smile,

For all the times you make me frown.

They make me feel like I mean something.

More than what I mean to you.

They want my attention.

They crave for me to give them my time.

ALL OF THEM - ALL OF YOU

And the sad part is,

What they want from me,

Is all I want from you.

SAVANNAH

I didn't know I could love a child,

Till my heart was introduced to you.

Then suddenly my world seemed much brighter.

I saw the innocence in your eyes and became scared of the future.

Scared this cruel world is too dark for an angel.

If I could give you anything in this lifetime, I would give you protection.

I never want to see you hurt, I never want to see you cry.

But, if I have to,

I want to be right there with you to hold you in my arms and tell you it will be okay.

I may not be your mother, but I'll love you like my daughter.

SAVANNAH

Being your aunt is the best gift life has blessed me with.

Now I get to walk through life sharing that with you.

The possibilities of this life I didn't know were true.

I now love a child,

Since my heart met you.

WHY SO TIRED?

I'm tired from not being able to sleep.

I can't sleep because my mind is always racing.

The race is about time, money, happiness and survival.

In order to survive I have to work.

I have to work as much as I can in order to make money.

But, if I work too much I burn myself out, and run out of happiness.

If I put my happiness first then I'll need to find the time to take care of myself.

But, how can I find the time, if all I do is work?

If I cut work time, I'll have less money.

If I have less money it will be hard to survive.

If I can't survive and can't pay my bills, how will I be happy?

WHY SO TIRED?

Do I work as much as I can so when I'm older I can retire and enjoy happiness?

Sacrifice my time and happiness to make enough money to be happy in the future?

What If I want to be happy now?

So, if I wait year after year until I get old enough to enjoy life with no struggles, would it be worth it?

Can you guarantee I won't get sick?

Can you guarantee as I grow older my bones won't grow older too?

Can you guarantee I'll still be able to do all the things I want to do now, then?

Can you guarantee I won't be in pain?

Can you guarantee I'll live to see the day where all my hard work pays off?

Can you guarantee by the time it all falls into place, I finally won't be tired?

This vicious cycle that became a circle of destructive thoughts is the reason I stay awake.

I'm tired of trying to find a balance between the things I have to do for survival and the things I have to do for happiness.

If you have to give up the pleasures that make you happy in order to survive is it even worth it?

I don't want to survive for the sake of being alive.

I want to be happy so I can live.

Live where I can go to sleep and wake up without being tired.

THE MENTAL CAPACITY OF UNSPOKEN THOUGHTS

Without being so tired of trying to survive.

SO TINY

Little tiny mouse.

What are you doing out of your field?

Finding food?

Finding warmth?

Finding shelter?

Trying to feed your family?

Little tiny mouse, just trying to survive.

Big scary human.

What are you doing out of your house?

Finding food?

Finding material to build up your home?

Trying to feed your family?

Big scary human just trying to survive.

We see a tiny mouse and consider them pests.

SO TINY

We can exterminate them because there are so many, and so small.

They are small because the world is so much bigger.

We are bigger.

Yet here we are.

Over populated, going on about our day to survive, just like them.

We play god and kill innocent creatures simply for doing what they are made to do.

We can get away with it, because they are so small.

But, then again so are we.

If we took the time to look up at the sky, we would realize we are tiny too.

Then what is the difference between us and them?

Little tiny mice, trying to survive until they can't survive anymore.

Big scary humans, the time will come when someone or something larger than us, greater than us, will come down and wipe us all away.

Then we will be considered tiny as well.

Just like them, we are all mice too!

A WRINKLE IN TIME

I'm sitting here blank, numb with just a stare.

Why is this happening? This news that broke isn't fair.

Unsure of my emotions, it's the sadness I can't bear.

Life would be much easier if I just didn't care.

This revelation breaks me, with reasons I try to find.

The truth is in my feelings, but I push it all aside.

You took life for granted, treated it like a ride.

We hear the click of the tick, as time's not on your side.

I'm sad because I care, when I know I shouldn't bother.

A figure you were supposed to be, my protector and my armor.

Chasing a relationship a daughter wishes to have with her father.

But, you never stepped up, and in time it just got harder.

I'm sad because I'm sinking in this boat you're supposed to row.

I'm sad because I love you, and I wonder if you know.

I'm sad this bond might end, and won't have the chance to grow.

I'm sad because I'm scared, I'm scared to let you go.

I'm scared for the results, I'm scared I have to wait.

I'm scared you won't escape, and meet heaven's gate.

I'm scared to watch you die, I'm scared to know your fate.

I'm scared to watch the clock, I'm scared that it's too late.

IMPOSTER SYNDROME

When people ask if we are close, I'm unsure of what to say.

I want to say yes, but in my heart I know that's not true.

I want to say yes because I know I light up your world (so you say).

But, as I light yours up, you tear mine down.

Does that make us close?

You think we get along, but that is only because you see a quarter of who I am. I know I can't be my authentic self, you wouldn't like her, believe me, I've tried. So I paint a picture of who you want me to be, just to have the relationship I always wanted to have with my father. Even if it is only for a little while. Even if she is an impostor. I grasp at the love the little girl inside of me always wanted. I cover up who I am, how I feel, what I think and what is true with a lie.

IMPOSTER SYNDROME

To appease you, so you can finally like me. If I showed you the truth, you wouldn't like me at all actually. I'm outspoken, brave, intelligent and more. I know my worth, I know my strength, and I'm always ready for a challenge.

But, you don't like to be challenged. You don't like strength because it reminds you of how weak you really are. You wouldn't like to know my worth because you would finally realize that everything you put me through, keeping you around would not be worth it at all. You wouldn't like my intelligence because it would remind you of your ignorance. You wouldn't like how brave I am because that would mean I am brave enough to stand up to you. And lastly, you wouldn't like how outspoken I am. This explains why you never showed interest in what I write. You refuse to hear or read the words about how I feel. My truth shines a light on your darkness. It shows who you are and what you will never be. Me being outspoken will only show you how I truly feel, and how I always felt.

You're scared of that story... scared of the truth.

So, instead I catch myself comforting you with a lie. To keep the peace. To keep this pretentious love.

Only to not break you.

To not break you, the way you have always broken me.

NOT SO FRAGILE

You're mad that you're soft, but did you know that if you're soft, you're strong?

You say you have a soft heart because you care too much.

You say you have a soft soul, because you feel too much.

You say you have a soft mind, because you think of others too much.

You're upset with yourself for putting yourself in their shoes to feel their pain.

To understand their pain, to accept and forgive the things they have done because of their pain.

Taking yourself out of your own skin to become someone else to understand their story takes strength.

Feeling sorry for others because you understand that there are layers to everyone's story takes strength.

Worrying about others and taking away from yourself to not be selfish takes strength.

NOT SO FRAGILE

You are open to the world around you, not drowning in the sorrows of your own existence.

You take from yourself to help others.

They come to you not because you're soft, they come to you to charge off your strength.

We are blinded by the terms others use to determine what weak and strength really means.

You're upset that you're soft, not realizing everyone perceives you as strong.

MONSTER

We're told monsters aren't real.

Since being children this is what we've learned.

I was once a human too,

Before the time I turned.

I'm not the monster that you think,

I don't hide under your bed.

I'm the monster from the cryptics.

I'm the one that wants you dead.

I'm not the imaginary monster in a story that you read.

I came here from a curse, now all I want to do is feed.

I can shift into a shape,

Whether it's an animal or a person.

I'll mimic a voice you know,

And you'll fall for it, I'm certain.

MONSTER

To get you where I need you,

I'll use all my tricks.

I'll lore you to the dark,

Where I'm hiding in the sticks.

I'm evil and I manipulate,

I'll confuse you till I win.

When you fall into my trap,

I'll sink my teeth into your skin.

They call me a myth, they call me a story.

They call me the mimicking stalker.

I have many looks, I have many names,

But, I'm best known as the Skin walker.

BLENDED PAGES

It's hard for me to read books.

And not because the words can be difficult to pronounce, or because the story doesn't grasp my attention.

It's not that the books are boring, nor is it due to me not having no interest at all.

It's hard for me to read books because I read books as if it's the last thing I will ever read.

The reason is, I seep into the chapters and become one with the story.

I get attached to the characters as if I personally knew them myself.

I become so engrossed with the literature that I can't hardly peel my eyes off the pages because I'm too deep into living in them.

I love books simply for the fact that it's my escape from the reality I breathe in every single day.

BLENDED PAGES

It's hard for me to read books because when the story ends, I feel as if I lost a part of me when closing the last chapter to every word I just read.

It almost feels like my story ended too.

SECRETS

When you look at me now, do you feel ashamed?

When you look in the mirror, is it you that you blame?

Did you think of my feelings during the act?

Or was it humanity, you started to lack?

Was it easy for you growing up knowing?

Did it ever cross your mind where this was going?

Did you hate me that much to cause me this pain?

Did you lie to yourself when you said it's a game?

Do you feel guilty that you caused me this harm?

Just a little girl, her innocents gone.

When you got older, did you think I grew up too?

Now that I'm older I struggle because of you.

I tend to make excuses for you and that shouldn't be.

The anger you had, you took it out on me.

SECRETS

When you decided to hurt me, did you think I'd be okay?

Did you think that this secret with us it would stay?

Yet till this day your hate shines through.

It's not you who should hate me, I should hate you.

You couldn't deal with your guilt for what you let be.

You found reasons to be ashamed and you took it out on me.

When you see me smile, do you still see fear?

Do you see disappointment when you are near?

When I get too uncomfortable I go off like a hinge.

And because of you, even with a hug I cringe.

The shame I feel, that this family got so bad.

Did you think I had fun? Or did you think I was scared?

Do you think I'm okay now? Because I am not.

Everything you did left my mind to rot.

But, you were also young and were abused yourself.

Every time you cried out, there was no-one to help.

Do you feel how I feel? In my shoes you didn't live.

But, your monster was Dads creation, so I can't help but to forgive.

DISTRACTION

I go to work as if it's a normal day.

Sit in my chair.

Take a deep breath, and whisper,

"Okay let's begin"

Notifications going off on my phone.

Terror happening all around the globe.

I flip my phone over, trying to ignore what I see.

My ear catches the radio playing behind me.

The talk of poaching animals in parts of the world.

I dread listening anymore, I plug my air pods in my ears.

Turn on music.

The lyrics that are blaring are raw, too raw for this day.

It just makes it worse.

Eyes fill up to the brink of waterfalls.

DISTRACTION

I can't escape the pain of reality.

I sit at my desk and wonder, as the world around me falls apart.

Why am I here?

MR. HAPPY

I'm depending on happiness.

I need it for the day.

The euphoric feeling,

My depression is stealing,

Turns the happiness away.

Without this crazed feeling,

My mood and expressions are drab, joyless, and formal.

The numbness dwells in me.

This way I hate to be.

I just want to finally feel normal.

But, what is normal, if normal is never found?

How can I know normal, when my head is in the clouds?

Mentally I'm struggling, I can't do it on my own.

I became a stranger to Mr. Happy.

MR. HAPPY

Now when I need him, he always comes over,

But only when I take an Addy.

I go from numb to happy, then happy to euphoric.

Then eventually I start feeling fine.

When the feeling wears off, and I'm stuck feeling lost,

It's then when I decide to do a line.

To live this way, sucks! I often lose hope.

To use horrible habits as a way to help cope.

And no one understands me, not my family, not my friends.

To reach the level of happiness, on drugs I must depend.

I'll only be understood when it's my funeral they attend.

When that day comes, I'll be done feeling numb.

And Mr. Happy is who I'll meet again.

I BURY ALL MY CHILDREN

This will not be my last heartbreak.

This will not be the last time I cry.

This sure as hell won't be the last time I feel like I'm capable of dying from a loss.

This empathy is something I will never escape from.

This is who I am.

This is how I was created.

And because of that, this will not be the last time I look into the mirror with my eyes beat red sobbing the words "this just isn't fair".

I will go on with life burying all of my children.

I will endure this forever pain, just to give each of my children a life filled with happiness.

They will never know pain, once in my arms.

They will never know fear, once in my heart.

They will never know abandonment, once in my home.

I BURY ALL MY CHILDREN

They will never know heartbreak, once in my life.

But, for them I will take that heartbreak over and over, if it means saving theirs.

I will do it for every wag, every meow, every bark, every sniff, and every lick.

And because of that, this will not be my last I love you.

This will not be the last of my tears.

This will not be my last goodbye.

SILENT

I'm screaming so loud.

But, my scream is silent.

There is no sound.

Unspoken words are violent.

You see me part my lips,

But, nothing seems to ring.

My voice is silent whips.

Which is why my quiet stings.

Yet my teardrops are so loud.

You hear them shatter with every drop.

They gas into a cloud.

Then you hear they've spoken up.

My voice shouts in silence.

A chirp less little bird.

SILENT

But, when I cry for guidance,
It's my tears that become words.

DISASSOCIATE

Depression creeps up when reality hits.

Isolating myself is an easier way to cope.

Spiritless I've been, lost in my own mind.

Analyzing every situation until it's fully dissected.

Sinking in my struggles.

Stressed about all the things I can't change.

Outburst all my rage that ends up in tears.

Collapse into myself, I am all that I have left.

In pain from the poison my mind feeds itself.

Anxious from all the racing thoughts.

Tired of the trauma that I can't escape from.

Empty for giving my all, till there's nothing left.

And when I disassociate, they scratch their heads and ask why…

DISASSOCIATE

Hmm… I wonder why?

OH HOW SHE LOVED HIM

Oh how she loved him…

The way that he spoke, the way that he walked, there was nothing he couldn't do.

It didn't take long for the words to be spoken and hear the endearing I love you.

He made her smile.

He made her laugh.

The memories made,

And photographs.

She loved his hair, and the feel of his skin.

She loved the roughness of his face when they kissed, on her chin.

There was nothing about him that she didn't love.

They were a perfect match, a fit like a glove.

OH HOW SHE LOVED HIM

With hand and hand,

Their fingers would curl.

She was his sky,

But, he was her world.

The love was overwhelming

For each other they carried.

Soon had kids, then soon became married.

They danced foot and foot, as songs played on and faded.

With a blink of an eye they became grandparents,

And a legacy between them created.

Together they were vowed, promised always and forever.

He left her messages as reminders of the love they shared together.

They were far from perfect,

But, imperfectly meant.

A life together, a long one was spent.

But, life for him ended so soon.

Her walls crashed down, her colors were gloom.

When he left this earth, he took a part of her with him.

THE MENTAL CAPACITY OF UNSPOKEN THOUGHTS

As she kept all the wonders of what could have been.

She tried to live, but would never move on.
Life without him was hard to go on.

He was not here, but he stayed in her mind.
It wasn't enough, but it wasn't her time.
She dreaded existing without him every day.
She wanted to be with him and on earth not to stay.
Just to hold him once more in her arms to lay.
She wanted to give up everything to go with him away.

As loved as she was, her place was not here.
She held on hard, but year, past after year.
We knew there would come a time where she needed to give up.
Her life with him shall continue, but with us it will stop.

Oh how she loved him…

As seasons change and rivers flow.

She needed him more than we needed her... so she finally let go.

CHOOSE

Would you still choose me,

If I showed you how I feel, when the smile falls off my face?

If I felt numb most of the time, but acted like I was okay?

If I spoke about all my doubts even if I'm sure where I stand.

If I explained all the, what if's I digest every single day?

If I yelled so loud my eyes would bulge and my veins would twitch?

If I told you how many times I wanted to disappear and never return?

Would you still choose me,

All the times I imagined driving so far away to never be found?

To run into the void without a trace left behind while wondering if you would miss me?

CHOOSE

Would you still choose me if it meant that I was unbearable at times with myself destructive thoughts that come to my head?

If it meant I would cry so much it would leave a puddle on your shirt?

If it meant I would question whether you were ever worth it?

For all the times I have shared my light with you, would you choose me at my darkest hour?

Or as the time eventually passes, would you choose to walk away?

HERE'S YOUR ANSWER

You question my change in attitude, I wonder why?

You question why I no longer care to be around you, but you forget that you taught me how to live with your absence.

You question why I'm distant, but didn't realize you pushed me away.

You question why I ran out of love, ignoring all the times I poured my love into you and got nothing in return.

You question why I cry, while blindly being the reason for my tears.

You tear me apart and interrogate my response to it.

The only answer I have is - I've finally given up.

TEASE

I tease you because the feeling of being wanted is something I have been missing.

I'm afraid once you have me, that the feeling of want you once held for me will suddenly disappear.

You will get me out of your system and no longer desire me again.

I tease you to keep you around.

Out of the fear of losing you.

MIRROR, MIRROR

I'm easy to get along with, sure cause I'm your mirror.

I look like me, but resemble you, can you see it now more clearer?

I become who you want, which is usually yourself.

Like picking out your favorite book clean right off the shelf.

Do you like swimming and sports? Sure! I do too.

Of course I like sushi dates, I'm your reflection, I thought you knew?

You want to be upset? I'll change my mood to also match.

Throw the same ball back and forth, I'm really good at catch!

MIRROR, MIRROR

Of course everyone likes me, I'm really tough to hate.

I mimic who you are and make your characteristics all my traits.

I rub you the wrong way? How could that be true?

That's strange how you feel, you don't like me, but I am you!

WHERE THERE'S SMOKE, THERE'S FIRE

All the ups and downs you put me through, my heart line officially flattened.

They question my sanity for all the fake news you spread about what really had happened.

You mentioned my reactions, but never the cause.

Made me into a villain, while you gather their applause.

The difference between us, I'd use my tears to put out your fire, I wouldn't have to re-think it .

But, if I were to burn and you had a glass of water I bet you would rather just drink it.

If they had to know the truth and hear your lies, it would be easier for you if I were dead.

WHERE THERE'S SMOKE, THERE'S FIRE

To make yourself feel better you would use my ashes to put a cross upon your own forehead.

I put up with your bullshit for all the times you had my mind so scattered.

I became so engulfed finally my anger turned flammable and into a hazard.

If they looked a little closer they all would notice the story you told them had stains.

But, they call you a hero for putting out my smoke, when in actuality you were the cause of my flames.

Aren't you so brave for all that you saved, following all of the sirens.

You fit your new role, you play the part so well, congrats for being a fireman.

DON'T SAY

You speak to me with so much confidence, as if your words match your actions.

You speak to me with a tone not knowing I'm familiar with that melody.

You speak to me with the understanding that I don't have a clue.

But, I do.

Don't say you care about me when you find little to no interest in what I care about at all.

Don't say you need me when all the times I've offered you a helping hand, you assume I'm playing the role of your mother.

Don't say you think about me when I call you throughout the day and you're annoyed by my presence.

Don't say I'm everything you need when you look at me as a simple replacement.

DON'T SAY

Don't say you want to spend the rest of your life with me if my absence doesn't affect you.

Don't say you love me when you know deep down I'm just a temporary habit.

You speak as if I'm stupid.

You speak as if I'm blind.

You speak as if your words have no effect on my vulnerable heart.

Your words are as transparent as a shallow puddle lying on the ground.

I can see right through your words.

I can hear the deceit in your voice.

You think I'm clueless but one day you will be humbled.

The day I humble you is the day I take your words and use them as a red carpet to help me walk away.

But, I'll never speak to you the way you speak to me.

The only words you will ever hear spoken is when my lips part to say the words goodbye.

WHERE DO WE GO?

When we come into this world from the second we are born.

Life with a connected soul and commandments we are sworn.

Learn to become human until god blows his horn.

Then we leave who we love, so the alive can start to mourn.

This process will happen over and over.

Some of us become woke to the awakened exposure.

She knew there was more beyond the earth and the solar.

Help from spirituality was the thing that drove her.

We were taught about economics, money, and the loan.

Taught to use a computer, a TV, and a phone.

They teach you not to believe in anything not shown.

Throw us in a dome and expect to call it home.

WHERE DO WE GO?

Until there's nothing left and our body turns to stone.

But, no not her as she's experienced the unknown.

They tell us what to do then tell us who to believe in.

There's so much with our eyes we are willingly not seeing.

They say there's a God and he's waiting in his garden.

When we are six feet underground with flesh and bones that are rotting.

They preach what they want because they're the ones that are plotting.

And we have sheep that are among us who just agree and keep on nodding.

We are made of energy, but this vessel has a brain.

We are filled with blood and veins and unfortunately feel pain.

They call the close minded strong and the open mind insane.

They want all to have equality yet preach we're not the same.

There could be a God more than one, and a hell.

There could be a heaven there are also other realms.

It's even possible to think we live in a world full of portals.

It's possible to think we could be more and immortal.

Maybe at the end we finally get to choose.

Where we want to go and what we want to lose.

THE MENTAL CAPACITY OF UNSPOKEN THOUGHTS

Possibilities are endless and that is okay.

Cause here on earth is not our forever stay.

Earth is not our home there has to be better.

Maybe when I'm gone on my wings I'll grow feathers.

Maybe I'll become a God or get to control the weather.

Or maybe I'll end up in heaven where we all end up together.

There's so much more to us, energy has many sides.

They call it life and death, but I call it just a ride.

Emotions stay with energy as we can smile, laugh, and cry.

Curiosity won't go away because it's important to ask why.

And for this world and our galaxy we don't ever say goodbye.

For spirituality as we see it we will never die.

When we leave this level it's our memories that we keep.

We will travel on to other places and we can go very deep.

We know there's so much more that our minds are willing to keep.

So answer me this question: where do we go when we sleep?

REMEMBER

When they hurt you in a constant pattern it's not something you should forget.

Keep those flashbacks in your pocket you'llneed them for the next step.

They will return and continue to use you, show you their back and want a scratch.

But, they never scratch yours leaving you with an itch and It's that energy you'll need to match.

Remember how they treated you, how they made you feel when you handed them the umbrella and got wet.

Remember when they stepped on you like a stone in a garden so their shoes don't get dirty, don't forget.

Remember all the times you gave an inch they took a yard, you would crawl, and they would over step.

Remember you were available even all the times they were absent, please don't ever forget.

REMEMBER

The opportunist of a user will lay at bay until it's time for them to be in the center.

When the center is open and they come knocking, throw that grenade back and remember.

Remember

Remember

Remember

I'M SORRY

You found me as a puppy, rescued me as a stray.

Fast forward seventeen years later, I'm sorry I couldn't stay.

You loved me unconditionally, fed me treats and let me play.

I know you loved me dearly, I'm sorry I couldn't stay.

My new dad became my hero, in his seat I'd always lay.

Mom, thank you for giving me a better life, but I'm sorry I couldn't stay.

I would tilt my head and listen to everything you had to say.

I know you miss me desperately, I'm sorry I couldn't stay.

When you rocked me in your arms, I would fall asleep to the sway.

You wanted me to live forever, but I'm sorry I couldn't stay.

I'M SORRY

I know when I got sick there wasn't any amount you weren't willing to pay.

To get the medicine I need I know you tried, but I couldn't stay.

If there was a choice to hold me for eternity you wouldn't have it any other way.

But, life is short and that couldn't be, which is why I couldn't stay.

You gave me everything you could offer, but I had to go away.

To be at peace and cross the rainbow, I'm sorry I couldn't stay.

You held on to me tightly even when my face was turning gray.

I will forever always remember you, I'm sorry I couldn't stay.

Thank you for giving me a second chance at life, I'm grateful for all the days.

Till the very end I felt important, but I'm sorry I couldn't stay.

I'm with you now forever, I hear you when you pray.

Until we meet again I'll wait for you in heaven where I'll stay.

ALL FOR NOTHING

I wanted to feel numb so when I was offered the drug my response was quick to take it.

A coping mechanism to help ease the pain is all I ever wanted.

I just wanted a break.

So, a break is what I took.

Walking around feels lighter than usual.

Inhaling the air feels cleaner too.

All of a sudden life didn't seem as bad anymore.

I wake up every day wondering how I escaped the madness.

Did one time really do the trick?

My happiness quickly dissipated.

I forgot what happiness is supposed to feel like.

I wanted to feel numb, but now the numbness has completely taken over.

ALL FOR NOTHING

I pretty much feel nothing at all.

Almost like I'm not here.

Almost like I don't exist.

Then it dawned on me.

That night when I gave into temptation and took the offer to feel empty, I didn't realize I took the offer to be emotionally paralyzed forever.

For the taste of peace I sold my soul.

It was only till now I realized the deprivation of sensation was the virtue of death.

I can't wake up, I can't feel alive.

Because I've been dead this whole time.

SELFISH DEMOLITION

She had her doubts, but tried swallowing them, she knew you deserved a chance.

You gave her everything she dreamt of, the fantasizing romance.

You took the time to get comfortable then you changed so fast.

You waited till she let you in to mislead and drop your mask.

You waited till she needed you thinking she's wrapped around your finger.

You use her vulnerability as a gun and to your convenience you pull the trigger.

You waited till she was deep, letting year pass after year.

Played with her abandonment you knew it was her fear.

You never put her first when you were all that she'd need.

SELFISH DEMOLITION

You gave her promises and rings to make her falsely believe.

You made her think that she is worthless and you think it's okay.

If you only knew what it took for me to become who I am today.

You took someone who I'm proud of and selfishly destroyed her.

Just to help yourself conscious needs and now you try to avoid her.

It took me years to build her up, it took me years to mend her soul.

It took me everything I had just for you to take it all.

Now I have to work on her again and this time it will take much longer.

But, I'll take my time and give her armor so next time she'll be much stronger.

MY DAUGHTER

When I have a little girl there's so much in this world I would deeply want for her.

I would want her to love all her flaws and understand flaws are what make you perfectly imperfect.

I would want her to love herself more than she can anyone else.

I would want her to experience pureness and have youthful memories of being a kid.

I would want her to have a father that is noble enough to look up to.

I would want her to laugh, dance, sing, and prance.

I would want her to be strong so she can handle what life may rip away from her.

I would want her to be empathetic and know it's okay to cry.

I would want her to receive innocent love notes that one day will turn into roses.

MY DAUGHTER

I would want her to appreciate learning and never be afraid to grow.

I would want her to know her worth and one day find someone who knows it as well.

Most of all I would want my daughter to know what happiness is and to never forget it.

For her to feel it, want it, and give it.

I would want her to know that I too learned to love myself and because of that I was able to be the best mother I tried to provide for her.

I would want my daughter to know the only person I love more is her.

And one day if she has a little girl I would want her to love her just as much as well.

ROAD TRIP

We're driving in silence.

Music turned off.

Voice boxes keeping silent.

This road is very long, miles upon miles and we notice it's starting to get dark.

The sun goes down, the stars come out and the wheels on this truck keep on spinning.

Nothing to be said. We only hear the air between us and it's thick from all the lingering tension.

I have words in my head that want to come out, but I can't get myself to speak.

This road is longer than we expected and we are both getting tired. You can see the exhaustion in our eyes.

ROAD TRIP

We are running out of gas, but hopelessly keep going, looking for a turning point in the road.

We glance at each other with a smug side eye back and forth from time to time.

The silence is so loud, you hear it so obviously spoken.

Speaking to us in our consciousness.

It's time we stop siphoning gas as it's clear this is where we pull over.

This is when we realize our road has come to an end.

A FAMILIAR PLACE

I closed my eyes

And fell asleep.

Moved onto a place

I see in my dreams.

I open them up

And can finally see.

That this is the place

Where I'm meant to be.

I've been missing emotions

The feeling of love.

So, I came to the place

That I've been dreaming of.

I float across

The Crystal Lake.

A FAMILIAR PLACE

Look down at the reflection

To see my own face.

Is this the place

Where I need to be?

Is this the place

Where I can freely be me?

There was a tree and

Her leaves were pink.

She turned to purple

Just as fast as I blinked.

The grass is soft

With magic roots.

Asked If I was hungry.

Then it grew me some fruit.

The air and wind

Have a melody.

That always plays

And gives me clarity.

This familiar place

I've been before.

Don't want to leave.

Please close the door.

This land I'm with

THE MENTAL CAPACITY OF UNSPOKEN THOUGHTS

Gave me the impression.

This place is meant for me

I think this might be heaven.

CHECK MATE

He imagined a perfect life, and it came with the snap of his fingers.

Got everything he wanted, but that greed would often linger.

He needed it all to be the one on top.

Never settled for much and loved the thrill to shop.

He adored the lavish life and all the name brand stores.

But, when it came to his heart he loved his ego more.

He needed the attention and got filled with ugly greed.

His ego needed more whatever it craved is what he'd feed.

He got everything he dreamed of, a wife with a family.

The picture perfect fence painted white living happily.

But, who's really happy? His wife or only him?

All the times her light was bright he would run to make her dim.

CHECK MATE

He needed her dull while he was waxed and shined.

To trap her in a life to make her think she's wined and dined.

Give enough to feed her fantasy so she won't run, just stand his side.

Hoping she wasn't smart and for him her eyes were blind.

Says he's on a work trip, spoon fed her lies right to the head.

When he's lying in a hotel room with a one night stand in his bed.

But, she's smarter than he thinks, she's already called his bluff.

She took all his bullshit and she's finally had enough.

While he's finishing the cherry that sat on top of his forbidden cake.

Soon when he came home he would realize his mistake.

He came home to a house that was hollow and rather empty.

Trying to figure out why but when it came to reasons she had plenty.

From putting up with lies and all the cheating it became exhausting.

So she packed up and left while he was on his knees licking frosting.

When he had his final crumb he was baffled, he never guessed.

THE MENTAL CAPACITY OF UNSPOKEN THOUGHTS

Whole time he was moving his checkers, his wife was playing chess.

WE ALL BLEED

I was born mixed race and since I was a little girl, I was hated by many for not being the race of their liking.

White people hated me because I was not all white.

Black people hated me because I had white in me.

Spanish people hated me because I wasn't all Spanish.

Urban culture thinks any amount of white in me, automatically makes me white.

White culture thinks because I have tan skin it automatically makes me black.

I had family who disliked me, called me an Oreo, called me a mutt.

At the age of nine I was confused why certain family loved my all white siblings/cousins more than me.

I became programmed to hate myself.

I used to beg for peach colored skin.

WE ALL BLEED

I used to cry for being born me.

Growing up I finally found confidence.

I started seeing who loved me not for my color, but for who I am inside my heart and my mind.

Now people pay to have my lips.

People pay tanning salons to have my skin.

People get perms to get my curly hair.

Everything that I hated I was, became something everyone wants that I am.

I guess that's the bitter sweet of being mixed.

Most people will like half of you, but the important people will love all of you.

I am not the color you see.

I am not the culture you think.

I am human.

So the one thing racism has taught me is if someone has a problem with who you are it does not confirm something is wrong with you.

It proves there is something wrong with them and how they were raised, and how they think.

For the people/so called family that has ever pushed me down because of

Who I am, I am not mad at you.

THE MENTAL CAPACITY OF UNSPOKEN THOUGHTS

I feel sorry for you.

I feel sorry that you grew up ignorant and didn't know how to properly love.

I feel sorry for you being so small minded that your own intelligence will bring you down and make your small world even smaller.

Black, White, Spanish, Asian, Native, European, Indian, Woman, Man, and Animal.

We all bleed the same color.

I WONDER

I wonder if you will ever be sorry.

Maybe when you are, it will be too late.

I wonder if you will ever recognize the pain you have always inflicted.

Do you know how many times I've cried myself to sleep wondering when you would finally wonder all you have caused me?

I didn't want it this way.

But, it seems like I'm the only one who can't escape you.

My mother left and never looked back.

Eventually my brother was set to follow.

Then there I was, hoping you would change.

Maybe if you saw everyone leave, you would eventually wake up and understand this whole time it's been you.

You look back at all you said and did while standing proud.

I WONDER

So, I stopped wondering about you.

Instead I decided it's time to wake myself up.

To escape.

Escape you, your abuse, and your horrors.

I had to teach myself to not worry about you anymore.

Stop myself from wondering if you wonder about me.

Instead of wondering, I wandered.

Into the light, into peace.

Into being free.

JAGGED MIND

I wonder what it's like to feel that you're protected.

But, it was fear you injected.

And your insecurities you projected.

To mold me into the person that you wanted perfected.

Not realizing all along it was my mind you affected.

You think that it's love when we are only trauma bonded.

Your answer was abuse, that's the way you responded.

A hero you were supposed to be, but a monster you became.

The only time you were descent is when it was pictured in a frame.

Put on a smile and act for the portrait.

All the trust I gave and somehow you lost it.

Poured love into your hands, you turned around and tossed it.

JAGGED MIND

The boundary I put up and all the times you crossed it.

Father of the year, you rigged that award.

Bragging to the neighbors to receive their applause.

Yet I feel sorry for you and show too much empathy.

No matter how much you impacted and distorted my memories.

You deserve no forgiveness, not a drop of my sympathy.

From all the hell you gave me I remember so vividly.

Your manipulation won't work, it's one thing I've outgrown.

The only reason why I feel bad, it's called Stockholm syndrome.

Karma's a bitch and with you I am finished.

Shedding tears for you, I learned to resist.

Just like you did with me, your emotions I'll dismiss.

The price you get to pay for being a narcissist.

YOUR FINALE

I write about my pain, it's the beginning of my healing.

In hopes that one day you'll read everything I'm feeling.

I gave you so many pages, almost a chapter in my book.

But enough is enough and enough is what you took.

So this will be my last and in time I'll get to heal.

This layer to our story is at its final peel.

I won't succumb to my trauma that was built from tears and rage.

All the conflict you endured this will be your final page.

I'm forced to turn my pain into anger to help forget you.

Shine my light on your darkness and speak what is true.

A child so empathetic and you cause her so much pain.

You say we look alike, but trust me, we are not the same.

YOUR FINALE

My goal was to be different, break the cycle of your game.

Witnessed everything you did and went against its grain.

Your abuse affected my animals, me, and my brother.

You controlled everything around you and pushed away my mother.

I was too little to speak up so I had to watch in horror.

A little girl grew up afraid of her father.

Then everyone left and I only stayed.

The only good times we had eventually would fade.

You didn't care who I dated even when they were twice my age.

A child who was groomed and yet you weren't fazed.

Walk in the door with bruises and black eyes.

You never asked questions or batted a concerning eye.

Walked passed me when I was sad, even when I cried.

The faith that you would change and soon my faith would die.

As I grew older I became more wise.

I left your home, but never your side.

With a shred of hope, hoping you'll change.

But, hoping was pointless as that day never came .

The arguments I had with you in my head kept me up all night.

You made me feel guilty for doing what's right.

THE MENTAL CAPACITY OF UNSPOKEN THOUGHTS

I cried so much the tears burned my face.

Hoping I can heal from all your mistakes.

You discarded all you did, all you ever put me through.

If heaven is real I wonder what it would look like for you.

I wanted you to listen to understand all I have been saying.

After all these years of fear and sadness you've been portraying.

Never once thanked me for all my love and for me staying.

So I hope on your knees you will fall and plead on praying.

You want forgiveness for your actions, but that is not my job.

It doesn't matter if I forgive you, at the end that's up to god.

This time will be my last writing words I waste on you.

I gave up thinking you could change, there's nothing I can do.

I closed your chapter in my story so I no longer have to suffer.

From the broken heart you gave me, I'm on the road to recover.

TRIALS OF A DOG

When you say you love a dog, you understand the weight that it carries.

You know the love is indescribable, incomparable, and undeniable.

We meet our heart dogs, our lesson dogs, our soul dogs, and our forever dogs.

They each fill a place in our lives where we need them most.

But, then you meet a dog that is everything to you, all at once and more.

For me that is Hunter.

I loved him the very second my eyes met his.

He filled every empty hole my heart had displayed.

He loved me in the light and even as much in the dark.

He is the dog that has taught me the most important things about life.

TRIALS OF A DOG

Patience, acceptance, forgiveness, and eternal love.

When the world became too much for me and ending it all was a possible solution,

My everything dog was the only reason why I stayed.

I couldn't bear the thought that if I ever left his world, he would spend every day for the rest of his life searching for me, looking for me.

Wondering why I never came home.

To love a dog so much that I would take the pain and heartbreak every single day if it meant to save them from experiencing that excruciating void.

I dread for the day to come when it's my turn to lose the only thing that ever kept me hanging on.

Loving a dog comes with unbearable heartbreak that one day we know we'll have to face.

We know that it will crush us and it will take a part of our soul, but we still do it anyway.

Dogs give us the ability to love with the understanding that in the end there will be heartache.

They leave us after what seems like a short while, so they can make room for others to experience the same love we once gave them.

We don't replace them.

But, we honor them, memorialize them, grieve for them, learn from them, never forget them, and live on because of them.

We learn to continue to expand our love till the day we can eventually meet them again.

HEAD IN THE CLOUDS

I smoked a strain called memory loss.

Hoping it would stand up to its obvious name.

But, as much as I smoked and as much as I inhaled,

My memory stood the same.

Forgetting is easier, but it seems to not be working.

I think they might have mislabeled this strain.

I wanted my lungs to engorge the expectations.

So when I'm finished I'd forget all the pain.

There is no medication for a broken heart, but smoking could be a great remedy.

To forget all the pain, to never feel the same, I'll smoke away all of my memories.

WHERE DARKNESS LIES

Don't take my kindness for weakness and play me as a fool.

I show you, what I show you cause this fool is playing you.

This smile on my face, you think it's kindness you're receiving.

But, weren't you ever taught that looks can be deceiving?

I'm not delicate like a flower, but more like a grenade.

One wrong slip or move and you'll be praying to be saved.

Imagine the devil you're fearing is doing god's work.

You can see a hint of deceitfulness,

WHERE DARKNESS LIES

You can see it in my smirk.

I can walk around with grace, yet make you feel somber.
They call me dark.
I call it smart.
But, to most I'm known as karma.

Capricorn is my symbol,
Sign of the devil in fact.
I'm protected by the saints,
And the evil got my back.

I'll make you think I'm dumb, when in fact I'm very smart.
Let me show you all my work,
All my work that I call art.

You'll hear my voice when least expected and I'll hit you where it hurts.
I'll dig up all your secrets and affect you with my words.

People like to use their hands,
Don't get me wrong, I'll use mine.
But, my favorite way to hurt you is to get inside your mind.

THE MENTAL CAPACITY OF UNSPOKEN THOUGHTS

When your head rests on that pillow, your thoughts will start to melt.

Cause I'll hit you where it hurts and I'll hit below the belt.

The weapon is my mouth,

Like a gun that just gets bigger.

My tongue is very sharp

And plays the role of the trigger.

I cock it back when I attack,

Can't take back what's said and done.

Your head blows off just from those thoughts

That I implanted and I won.

Pray to the god you so adore.

It's already done and seen before.

Hypocrite is what you are, a walking contradiction to the core.

You want to take yet never give, crave attention, but you ignore.

Preach the lord's book with his oaths that you swore.

They all hand you their cup,

But it's hate that you pour.

Then when evil comes back to you, you wonder what for.

But, you decided to wake me up and you can't handle what's in store.

You want forgiveness, but I want war.

Your begging stop, but I want more.

You want your actions to go unnoticed, the quiet steps that walk the floor.

But, you get what you deserve when you knock on the devil's door.

HABIT

They say it takes two weeks for your body to adjust to a habit.

I met you and two weeks later you said you couldn't imagine never having the chance of meeting me.

We spoke every day, you got used to my song and kept it playing on repeat.

We saw each other so frequently you decided you needed to wake up to my face every day.

I gave you a key, we role played house and you got used to the "traditional" life.

But, now when you look at me, I see routine emotion, like something you're already simply used to.

You convince yourself that it's love because you're used to a warm body and grew tired of being used to the feeling that you got when you were alone.

You say that you love me, but it was your fear of solitary that turned me into a habit.

HABIT

A repetitious drug that makes you think it's love, thinking you're addicted and you can't live without it.

DREAM WORLD

I walk this world when I'm awake, but when I sleep I love to travel.

When I get tired of this world, I close my eyes to change the channel.

To explore other realms we can't see with the naked eye.

Other worlds we don't experience at least not until we die.

It's a gift I have been given to peek behind the curtain.

A glimpse to endless chapters of worlds of different versions.

I have been to worlds that were nightmares, had me scared and left me shaken.

I walked in worlds that were so beautiful, my breath was simply taken.

I've gone to heaven, went to limbo, I've witnessed death and witnessed birth.

DREAM WORLD

I've been to hell, but so have you because the devil plays on earth.

I'm no stranger to the unknown, I've been there plenty with my spirit.

When the real world gets too heavy, I close my eyes to escape and visit.

I don't travel when awake. It's when I sleep I become an explorer.

An ability to other dimensions, I've been granted the dream walker.

MY DESTINATION

I'm going on a journey to a place I need to be.

I've waited for so long and I've waited patiently.

I'm excited for my trip, I hope I get there soon.

The only map I need to follow is the light of the moon.

My friend is waiting for me, they'll be there when I arrive

It's been so long since I saw them, I've been waiting all this time.

They have been waiting for a while till my dates on earth expired.

Now my soul is ready, down on earth I grew tired.

I'm at my half way point, I cross a bridge with many colors.

With names that are engraved from the loss of many others.

MY DESTINATION

I see the paw prints on the pavement as proof of past existence.

I hear the echoes from all angels barking in the distance.

I ran to the entrance from excitement. I can't hardly wait.

Before I fully get there, I see him at the gate.

I step off the bridge to bright lights with strobes of flashing.

He notices me right away, I can see his tail is wagging.

Beyond him I see much more, animals at peace in heavens farms.

I fall down onto my knees, he runs and jumps into my arms.

Together for eternity, he will never be alone.

I crossed the rainbow bridge, now together we are home.

LOST AND FOUND

I think the problem with me is, I love people who will never love me the way I love them. I talk about cousins like siblings, but the truth is it is never reciprocated. I reach out to people in hopes they would do the same. But, that is a hopeless hope as that day will never come. I include everyone I love with the desire they will also include me. I'll use up all my time just for them to have no time for me at all. I make myself available no matter how much exhaustion I'm feeling, I can always find the time to sleep. Unfortunately the second they yawn I become a burden. I treat them fairly, but I'm treated without a fair thought in mind. I become a people pleaser, so I can also be seen as a person. A person who just wants to be reciprocated in the love and energy they put into others. But, as soon as I match their energy my title becomes a bitch, petty, argumentative, and sensitive. That's when I realized those people are a lost cause. They are a lost cause, because they are lost themselves. And while they are lost, they hate the fact I have always been found.

FRENEMY

God himself needed a helper to punish those who he can't handle.

She was created in his image, but the name they chose was devil.

He gave the devil her own domain, to control the darkness here on earth.

He did not cast her out from abandonment, more like to help do his dirty work.

We destroyed the world he gave us no matter how much he tried to save it.

Yet we blame God for all the disasters that the world itself created.

God gave us grace, he gave us life, he gave free will, and all his best.

The devil's here to keep us humble, she brings karma, and brings us death.

He gave us water, gave us food, everything he gave was freely handed.

But, we took the life he gave us and we took it all for granted.

The amount of humans that lack empathy in humanity, its evil they portray.

Wildfires, and Catastrophic disasters, it's a price we get to pay.

God gave his light to all the darkness, to keep the evil away from winning.

And by that he has his help, but it's the devil that does his bidding.

THE WORST DAY OF MY LIFE

You wake up late for work, spill your coffee, get stuck in traffic, miss your meeting, get stuck in the rain, lose your wallet, and it becomes the worst day of your life.

We all get days that feel worse than others.

When I have a bad day, to me it's just a bad day.

Even if it's worse than the day before.

I know what the worst day of my life will feel like even though it hasn't come yet.

But, I know it's coming.

I don't know when, and I'm not sure if I want to know when.

It might make it hurt even that much more.

When the worst day of my life comes knocking at my door, I will have complete dread to open it.

I don't want to open it.

I never wanted to even hear that knock.

THE WORST DAY OF MY LIFE

But, it will invite itself in anyway.

I will be nothing, but empty and probably want to die.

I won't be able to eat or be able to sleep.

I will just sit on the floor, sob and cry.

The day that it comes, I will be devastated, inconsolable, uncontrollable, and broken in every way.

That day I will lose my faith, blame God, andscream into the sky for hours.

I won't understand and will look for justification on why this happened to me.

Even though I knew that day would come, I still will constantly question it.

There is no preparation for the worst day of my life, no matter how much I try to prevent it.

The worst day of my life hasn't happened yet, but when it does I will remove his collar.

I will keep it with his toys and all his favorite things, next to his picture.

I will cry from the pain and my life won't be the same

That day will be the worst and I'll wish it never came.

I STUMBLE

I tried to hate you.

I thought maybe if I convinced myself that I hated you it would be easier for me to let you go.

So every time I spoke about you, I reminded myself to speak about all the things that I hated you for.

When I thought about you, I thought of every reason to justify my hate.

But, as soon as I talk to you I stumble on my anger, and forget about the hatred I wanted to take place.

It didn't seem to work.

Asking myself why it is so hard to hate someone who simply deserves it?

Maybe that's because it's just not who I am.

I am not filled with hatred.

I often confused it with pain.

I STUMBLE

It's pain that I feel. But, hate?

I don't think I can.

Even though I should, I don't.

As much as I try.

I can't.

THE HUNT OF AN INNOCENT DEER

The deer looked so fragile, she was pure and walked with grace.

The hunter locked eyes on his target for him to track her down.

The hunter did what he does best, plan to set a trap.

For the deer to innocently be chased right into it.

He was smarter all along, he saw this fawn as naive.

He fed me crumbs to my liking and quietly set his trap.

His actions were intentional, he knew I was just a kid.

He devoured and had his way with me, experimenting with my innocence.

I knew it was wrong the moment my stomach felt that pit.

I was too young to understand what instincts were.

I was too young to understand that my instincts would protect me.

THE HUNT OF AN INNOCENT DEER

I didn't know I was being hunted.

I didn't know I was being abused until I learned the definition.

Consent was not an option for me, a child myself only understood attention.

I was given what every child wanted as an exchange for my hunters' sick pleasure.

I wanted his attention, but instead he used it to groom me.

I wanted to feel mature, but he did that by stealing my innocence.

I wanted him to touch my heart, but instead he touched my body.

I thought it meant that I was special, only to find out that it was rape.

My hunter wore his camouflage so well, so well I didn't see him.

Shot me with a silencer and made sure it kept me silent.

Lied there in a panic as life drained from my eyes.

When he finished his hunt he put my body down slowly.

Walked away with his earnings now I'm nothing, but a trophy.

SPIRITUAL WARFARE

There's a spiritual warfare here on earth.

Where evil is taking over and the good is getting hurt.

Every day we wake up to learn it's only getting worse.

Evil's been unleashed and we can't seem to break the curse.

Angels walk among us, but just as many demons.

They look so much alike because the form they take is human.

Now we fight hand and fist, this will be a bloodshed battle.

Some will be used as bait they call that group the cattle.

People now think backwards, we turned our morals into politics.

Care about the globe then think we're climatologists.

Hate the facts shown in front of us, but decide to blame the scientist.

SPIRITUAL WARFARE

We want a better world, but take no actions, just desire it.

The angels fold their hands, kneel, plead and pray.

For a better world to live in, to exist in everyday.

Dark entities seem to laugh, they think that we won't make it.

They want the dark to overrule and by force they want to take it.

The dark thinks they won, betting this war won't take much longer.

But, he forgets the power of good, he forgets that God is stronger.

The angles come together to gather all the good in people.

They use it as a weapon to defeat and conquer evil.

We fight for what is right, whether in our past we were saint or sin.

God has our back and because of that, this war we will win.

THE GIFT

I was born with a gift many others may find skeptic.

To see things that are hard to explain with messages I'm blessed with.

I can use both good and evil with the knowledge not all is black and white.

My purpose is to look for answers to prove what's false and right.

Some cherish my blessing, some lift a curious brow, some have voiced their fear.

Some think I'm a rebel that made a deal with the devil, which is why they think I'm here.

They couldn't be more wrong.

Of course I'll choose God, I'm his child in the end.

THE GIFT

The devil was once an angel, that's why he and God are friends.

The lord gives me his strength, that's the reason I'm his light.

I'm no foe to the darkness, for reasons why I thrive at night.

Some think it's not a blessing that I have been gifted with a curse.

But, if the curse is a gift, which one is considered worse?

I'm made up of them both, I have many different sides.

I can be the greatest friend or enemy, depends on who you decide.

I was put on this earth to observe this crazy man made circus.

I'm here to spread awareness of my gift I call my purpose.

I'm here to wake you up, to prove we're not alone.

I'm here to bring a message that there's more to the unknown.

WALKING AMONG US

You spend your whole life helping others when you do so little for yourself. But, tell me this….

When this life is finally over and you are offered the chance to experience life over again, would you do things more differently?

If your answer is no it is because you were not put on this earth to live.

You were put on this earth to help others survive.

That's your purpose.

Some people think angels come in the form of a spirit and many do.

But, then there are angels like you who chose to be here, who chose to help others.

You are an angel that chose to walk among us.

DEATH IS NOT THE ANSWER

You say you want to die, but is it death that you really want ?

You say you don't want to live, or is it the joy of living you really wish to feel?

Do you want the pleasure of not existing?

Or are you tired of people not noticing you exist?

Do you want to feel transparent where you feel nothing at all?

Or are you tired of feeling dismissed never knowing what it feels to be wanted?

Do you want to go to sleep and close your eyes forever?

Or are your eyes tired of fighting to stay awake?

DEATH IS NOT THE ANSWER

Do you want your body to turn cold and your heart to stop beating?

Or do you want to feel the warm comfort that your heart aches to feel?

Do you want to be buried and quickly forgotten?

Or do you just want to know if you will truly be missed?

Do you want your loved ones to move on and not care?

Or do you want to know who will shed genuine tears for your death?

You want to know if your existence matters, if your existence would be a devastating loss.

If validation is what you need to keep you alive, would you accept it and promise to stay?

THE PRINCESS AND THE WOLF

One mother raised a little girl to be a princess and my mother wanted the same.

The other little girl became the wanted princess, but a wolf is who I became.

The princess had innocence, carried with daintiness, was pure to the bone underneath.

But, I was more stone with a strong backbone, raised with a sharp tongue and sharp teeth.

Growing up to be a princess was every girl's dream and she wanted to be the one who's sweeter.

But, I wanted to be intelligent, someone you can't reckon with. In my blood I was meant to be a leader.

Wolves are too complicated to deal with, the princess is more convenient.

THE PRINCESS AND THE WOLF

They want to fill a world with easy yes girls, but I never wanted to be it.

The princess looked down on me and thought she was above me, didn't care how I was treated.

But, now we live in a world where survival is primal and now it's the wolves that are needed.

Where territorial and relentless and are very proud of both.

My mother wanted a princess, but instead she raised a wolf.

US AND THEM

We love to compare ourselves to animals, until it's time to acknowledge how we treat the ones we compare ourselves too.

They kill to eat in order to survive.

So do we.

They can be very unpredictable.

So can we.

They can't be fully trusted.

Neither can we.

They are dirty and carry disease.

So do we.

They can be dangerous in packs.

So can we.

They can relocate somewhere else.

US AND THEM

So can we.

But, we are humans who can feel pain.

So can they.

We have emotions.

So do they.

We have families and children.

So do they.

We just want to be free.

So do they.

We want to live.

So do they.

We are capable of love.

So are they.

You know what they can do that we can't... Co exist.

ILLUSION

Can you imagine if we found out life was an illusion?

But, they spared us from the truth just to save us from confusion.

I wonder what you'd think if you found out we're not real.

That this life does not exist, I wonder how you'd feel?

If this is all just a creation, for a cell to have sensation.

The feeling of life and devastation that were created from imagination.

We all play the main character in our own lives, of this life's very own movie.

I'm no one to anyone, who at one time in this illusionary life once knew me.

All the memories we make and all the shit that we take.

We struggle everyday just to find out it's all fake.

ILLUSION

If this was nothing all along and we were living in a scheme

We were created by illusion of an eternal fucked up dream.

We would have wasted our time to care for all unanswered prayers.

When we struggled to prepare for our heaven in the air.

We leave behind nothing, but if nothing once was something.

Then this whole time there was nothing ever there.